W9-DGE-177

FUN WITH THE BARITONE UKE

MEL BAY

CD CONTENTS

This book is available either by itself or packaged with a companion audio and/or video recording. If you have purchased the book only, you may wish to purchase the recordings separately. The publisher strongly recommends using a recording along with the text to assure accuracy of interpretation and make learning easier and more enjoyable.

1 2 3 4 5 6 7 8 9 0

Visit us on the Web at www.melbay.com — E-mail us at email@melbay.com

Tuning the Baritone Uke

The four open strings of the Baritone Uke will be of the same pitch as the four notes shown in the illustration of the piano keyboard.

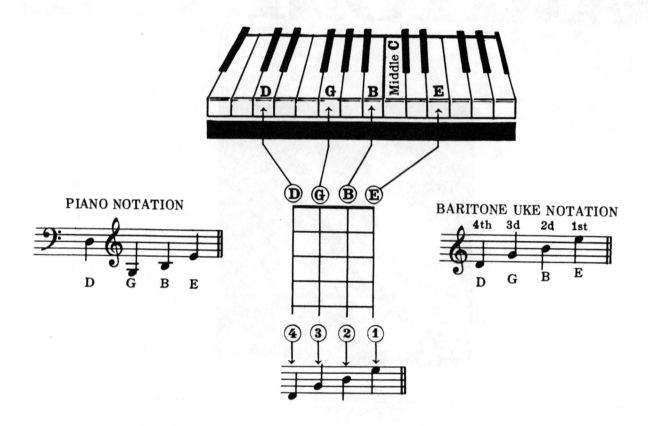

PIANO NOTATION

BARITONE UKE NOTATION

Another Method of Tuning

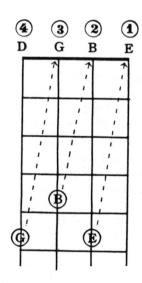

Place finger behind the fifth fret of the 4th string to get the pitch of the 3rd string (G).

Place finger behind the FOURTH FRET of the 3d string to get the pitch of the 2d string. (B)

Place finger behind the fifth fret of the 2d string to get the pitch of the 1st string. (E)

Pitch Pipes

Since there are no pitch pipes available at this time for baritone ukes, it is advisable to purchase a set of Spanish guitar pitch pipes and by eliminating the fifth and sixth string tones you will have the pitch of the baritone uke strings.

The Correct Way To Hold the Baritone Uke

This Is the Pick

Hold it in

this manner $\longrightarrow$

firmly between the

thumb and first finger.

Use a felt pick.

THE LEFT HAND

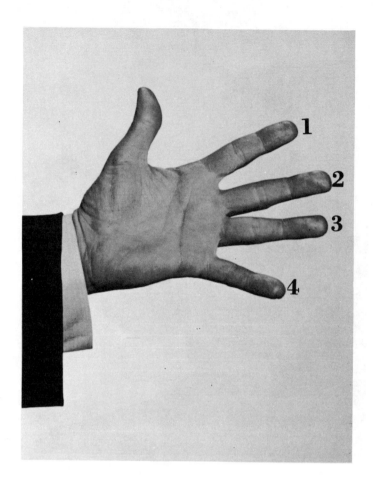

Practice
holding
the Uke
in this
manner.

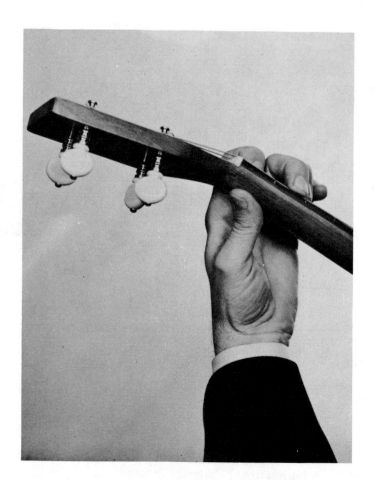

Keep palm
of the hand
from the
neck of the
instrument.

THE FINGERBOARD

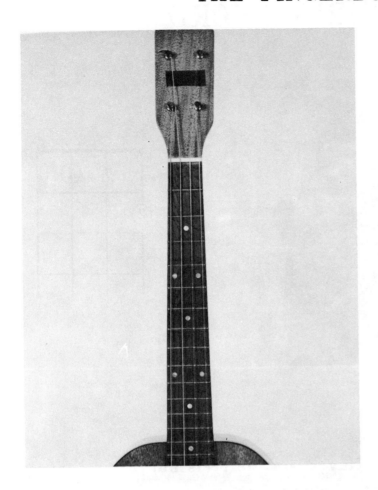

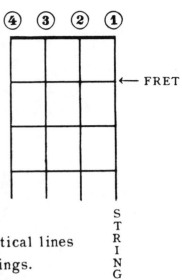

The vertical lines are the strings.

The horizontal lines are the frets.

The encircled numbers are the number of the strings.

Striking the Strings

⊓ = Down stroke of the pick.

OUR FIRST CHORD

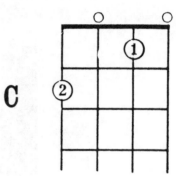

C

Do not place fingers on the frets but
directly behind them.

Do not apply too much pressure.

Practice the above Chord until the tone is clear.

/ / / / = Strokes of the Pick over the Strings.

/ / / = Strum the C chord three times in succession.

TIME SIGNATURES

$\frac{4}{4}$ or C = COMMON TIME

Hold the C chord and play it in this manner:

C   C   C   C

$\frac{4}{4}$ / / / /   / / / /   / / / /   / / / /

$\frac{3}{4}$ = THREE-FOUR or WALTZ TIME

Hold the C chord and play it in the following manner:

C   C   C   C

$\frac{3}{4}$ / / /   / / /   / / /   / / /

$\frac{2}{4}$ = TWO-FOUR TIME

Play it in this manner:

C

$\frac{2}{4}$ / /   / /   / /   / /

THE G7 CHORD

G7

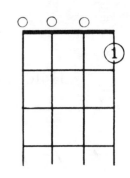

Play the C and G7 chords in the
following manner:

C	C	G7	G7

$\frac{4}{4}$ / / / /   / / / /   / / / /   / / / /

C	G7	C	G7

/ / / /   / / / /   / / / /   / / / /

C	G7	C	G7	C	G7	C

/ / / /   / / / /   / / / /   / 𝄽 / 𝄽

←REST→

𝄽 = Rest.   It indicates a period of silence.

See "BARITONE UKE CHORDS"
by MEL BAY

OUR FIRST SONG
(Using the C and G7 Chords)

Long, Long Ago

Be sure to play the
chords directly on each word or
syllable as indicated.

10

Down In The Valley

* Continue playing the C chord until you reach the G7 chord.
  Play G7 until you arrive at C.

Skip To My Lou

* No chord strokes on words in parenthesis ( ).

Buffalo Gals

Oh, My Darling Clementine

There will be no playing on the pick-up notes
at the beginning of the above song.

For More Fun See FUN WITH FOLK SONGS
by Mel Bay

THE "F" CHORD

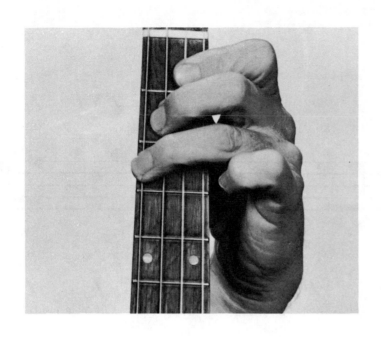

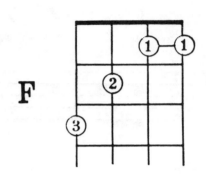

Master the following Chord Study:

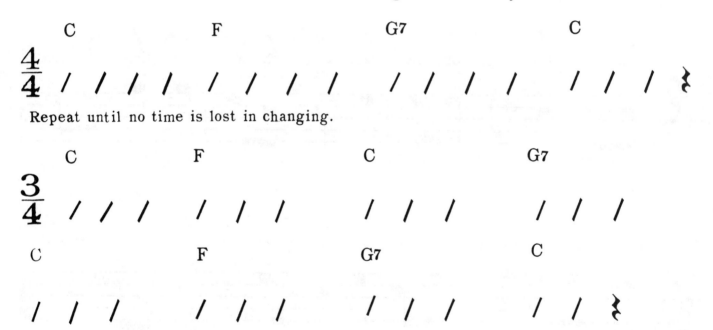

Repeat until no time is lost in changing.

The C, F and G7 chords are the principal chords in the Key of C.

See "BARITONE UKE CHORDS"
by MEL BAY

The Blue Tail Fly

* ⌢ = Hold the note extra long as in a pause.

For More Fun See FUN WITH FOLK SONGS
by Mel Bay

16

On Top Of Old Smoky

The Marines Hymn

There Is A Tavern In The Town

* The Pick-up note may be played by striking the third string open.

**For follow-up chord and strum techniques,
see FUN WITH STRUMS — BARITONE UKE**

* Strum the pick over the chord slowly
as in a harp style and let it ring.

THE D7 CHORD

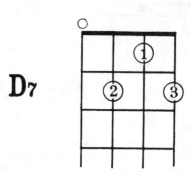

Play the following Chord Study:

	C	D7	G7	C	

C / / / / / / / / / / / / / / / ⸘ (REPEAT)

	C	D7	G7	C	

3/4 / / / / / / / / / / / ⸘

	C	D7	G7	C	D7	G7	C	C	

2/4 / / / / / / / / / / / / / / / ⸘

Master the above study before proceeding.

For supplementary chord studies,

See "BARITONE UKE CHORDS"
by MEL BAY

Our Boys Will Shine Tonight

(Introducing the D7 Chord)

In the last measure play the bass note on the first beat,
rest and play the C chord on the third beat.
The fourth beat is silent.

THE G CHORD

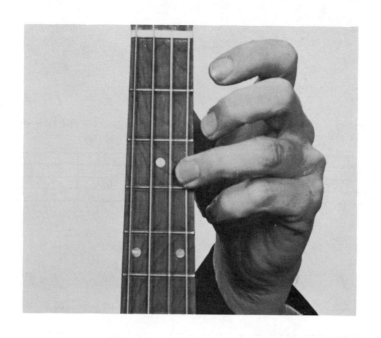

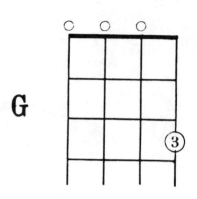

G

○ = Open String

The chords in the Key of G are: G, C and D7.

Play the following Chord Study:

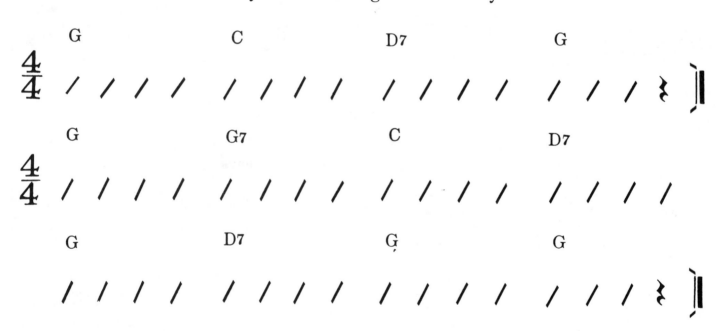

The Old Grey Mare

For More Fun See FUN WITH FOLK SONGS
by Mel Bay

She'll Be Coming Round The Mountain

Hand Me Down My Walking Cane

In order to start your song in the correct key,
strum the principal chord lightly before beginning.
In the above song the principal or tonic chord is G.

Red River Valley

SOME MORE CHORDS

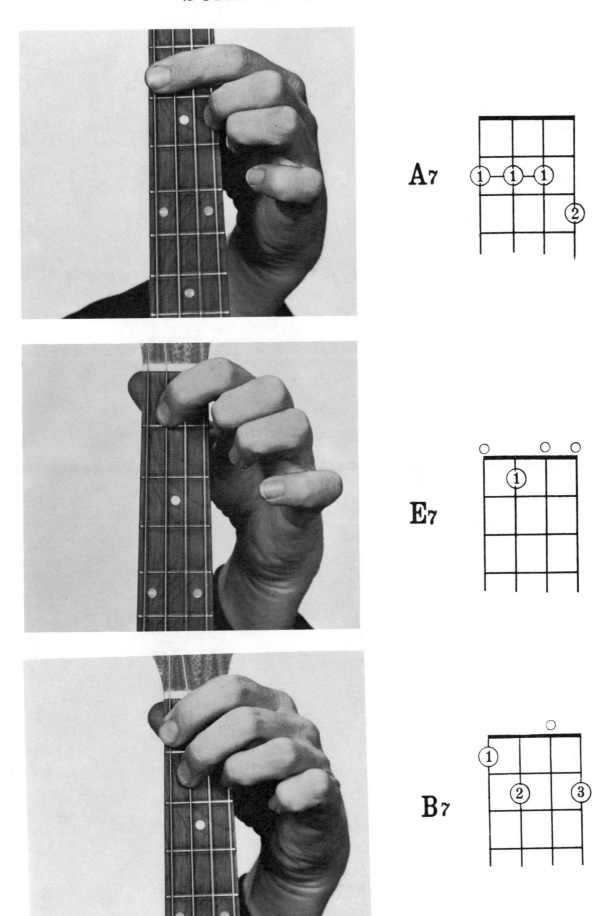

A7

E7

B7

For follow-up chord and strum techniques,
see FUN WITH STRUMS — BARITONE UKE

FUN WITH CHORDS IN "C"

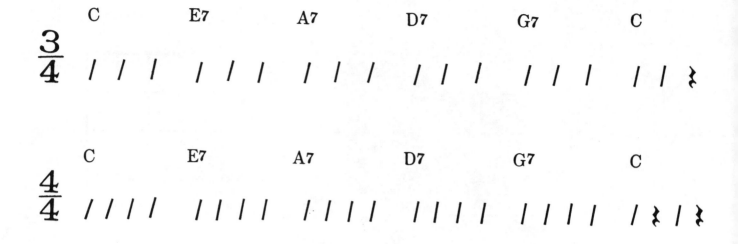

MORE FUN WITH CHORDS IN "G"

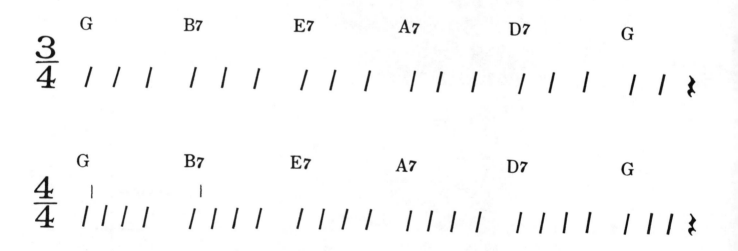

See "BARITONE UKE CHORDS"
by MEL BAY

Home on The Range

I've Been Working On The Railroad

In The Evening By The Moonlight

In the above song
strm the chords slowly.
For More Fun See FUN WITH FOLK SONGS
by Mel Bay

THE D CHORD

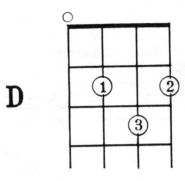

D

D	G	A7	D
$\frac{4}{4}$ / / / /	/ / / /	/ / / /	/ / / /

D	G	A7	D
$\frac{3}{4}$ / / /	/ / /	/ / /	/ / ‹

D	B7	E7	A7
$\frac{4}{4}$ / / / /	/ / / /	/ / / /	/ / / /

D	D7	G	D
/ / / /	/ / / /	/ / / /	/ / / ‹

Darling Nellie Gray

My Bonnie

Little Annie Rooney

For More Fun See FUN WITH FOLK SONGS
by Mel Bay

Oh! Susanna

Good Night Ladies

A CHORD SUMMARY FOR REFERENCE
The Major Chords

I

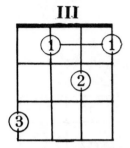

Frets	1	2	3	4	5	6	7	8	9	10
Chords	F	F# or Gb	G	Ab	A	Bb	B	C	C# or Db	D

Note: Each Form must be thoroughly mastered before proceeding to the next.

III

Frets	1	2	3	4	5	6	7	8	9	10
Chords	C# or Db	D	Eb	E	F	F# or Gb	G	Ab	A	Bb

V

Frets	1	2	3	4	5	6	7	8	9	10
Chords	Bb	B	C	C# Db	D	Eb	E	F	F# Gb	G

The Minor Chords

Im

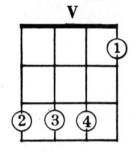

Frets	1	2	3	4	5	6	7	8
Chords	Fm	F#m or Gbm	Gm	Abm or G#m	Am	Bbm	Bm	Cm

IIIm

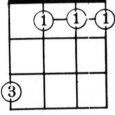

Frets	1	2	3	4	5	6	7	8
Chords	Dm	Ebm or D#m	Em	Fm	Gbm or F#m	Gm	Abm or G#m	Am

Vm

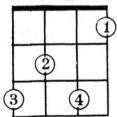

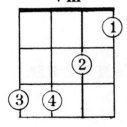

Frets	1	2	3	4	5	6	7	8
Chords	Bbm	Bm	Cm	Dbm or C#m	Dm	Ebm or D#m	Em	Fm

For follow-up chord and strum techniques, see FUN WITH STRUMS — BARITONE UKE

THE SEVENTH CHORDS

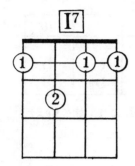

I⁷

Frets	1	2	3	4	5	6	7	8	9	10	11
Chords	F7	F#7 Gb7	G7	Ab7	A7	Bb7	B7	C7	C#7 Db7	D7	Eb7

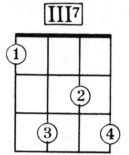

III⁷

Frets	1	2	3	4	5	6	7	8	9	10	11
Chords	Eb7	E7	F7	F#7 Gb7	G7	Ab7	A7	Bb7	B7	C7	C#7 Db7

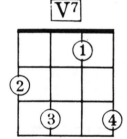

V⁷

Frets	1	2	3	4	5	6	7	8	9	10	11
Chords	C7	C#7 Db7	D7	Eb7	E7	F7	F#7 Gb7	G7	Ab7	A7	Bb7

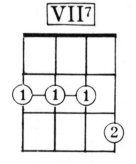

VII⁷

Frets	1	2	3	4	5	6	7	8	9	10	11
Chords	Ab7	A7	Bb7	B7	C7	C#7 Db7	D7	Eb7	E7	F7	F#7 Gb7

See "BARITONE UKE CHORDS", A COMPLETE

CATALOG OF BARITONE UKE CHORDS IN PHOTO-DIAGRAM FORM.